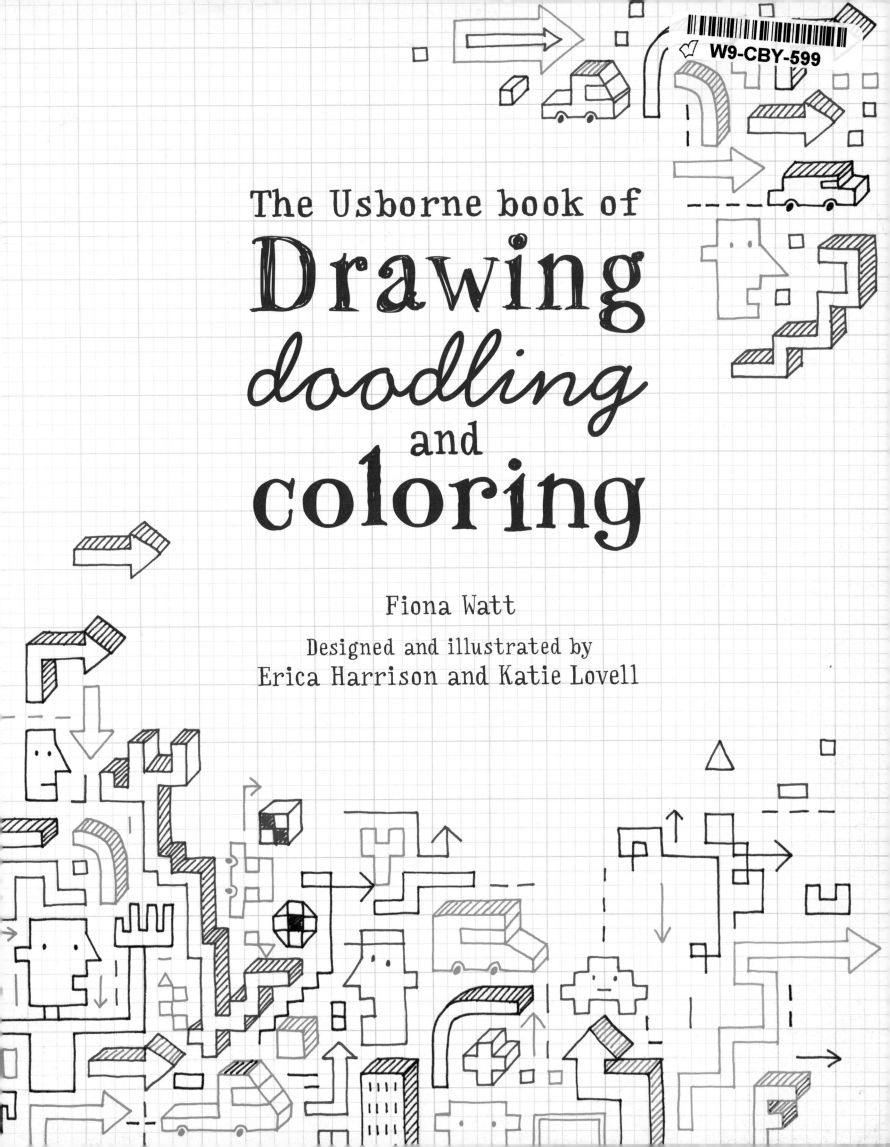

The Usborne book of
Drawing
doodling
and
coloring

Fiona Watt

Designed and illustrated by
Erica Harrison and Katie Lovell

How to use this book...

On some of the pages you'll find ideas for what to do, but you can do whatever you like.

Use pens, pencils or crayons to complete the pictures.

You could fill in large areas, or add stripes, spots or patterns of your own.

When you draw on top of a shape with a pen, wait for a couple of seconds for the ink to dry, so that it doesn't smudge.

Fill in some of the shapes.

Doodle more flowers and insects flying around.

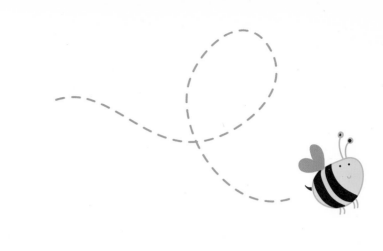

Complete the robots below, then doodle some more.

Draw more houses, trees, bushes and fences.

Turn these shapes into faces.

Fill the fishing boat's net with its catch.

Doodle more clouds, stars, planets and birds.

Doodle more spiders and flies.

Draw more monsters...

Doodle amazing wigs on the actresses and actor.

Fill in the butterflies
so that each one has
two wings the same.

Fill the buildings and roofs with lots of patterns.

Doodle on the snails' shells and add some slimy trails.

Doodle what you think might be stored in the jars.

Draw lots more bees...

Doodle eyes, mouths and teeth on these plants
and add lots of flies about to be trapped.

Design some dresses and accessories.

Draw more penguins on the ice.

Doodle your ideal meal or one you'd hate to eat!

Draw pictures in the frames.

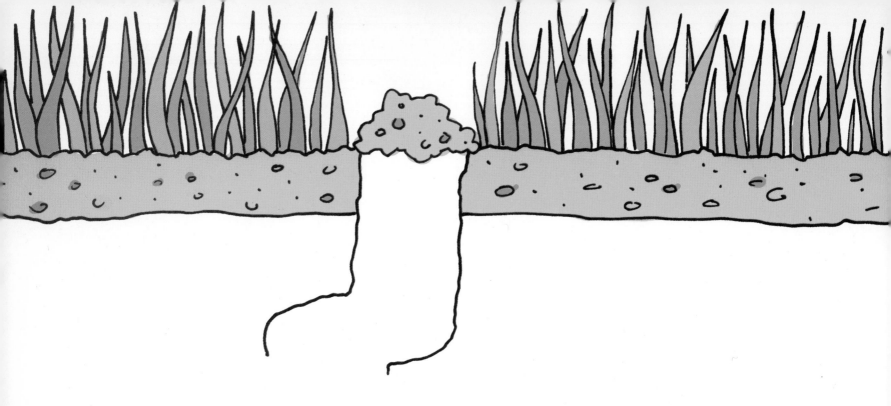

Doodle lots of things buried under the ground.

Doodle patterns on
the shells.

Draw more traffic on the busy roads.

Draw scary things in the windows and more bats fluttering around.

Turn these shapes into bugs.

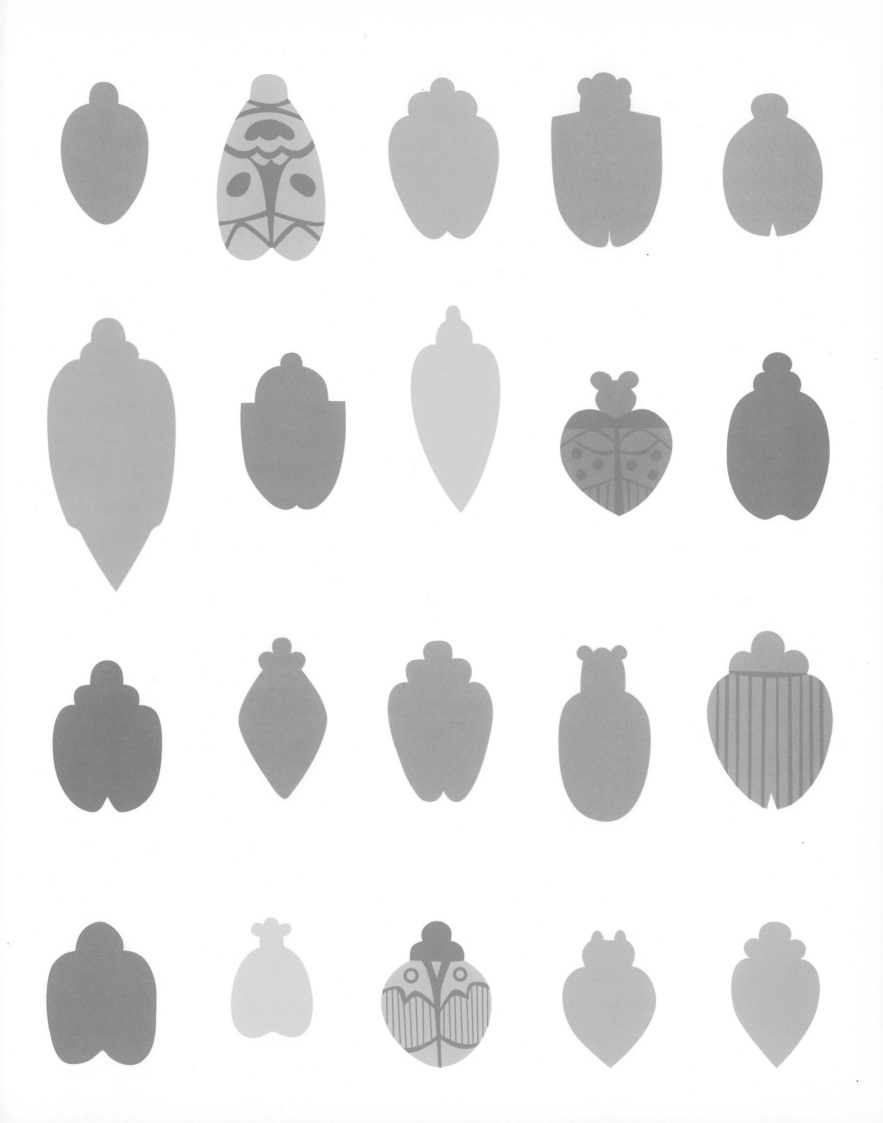

Doodle windows and draw more trees, buildings and clouds.

Draw birds first,
then draw over the
lines of the cages.

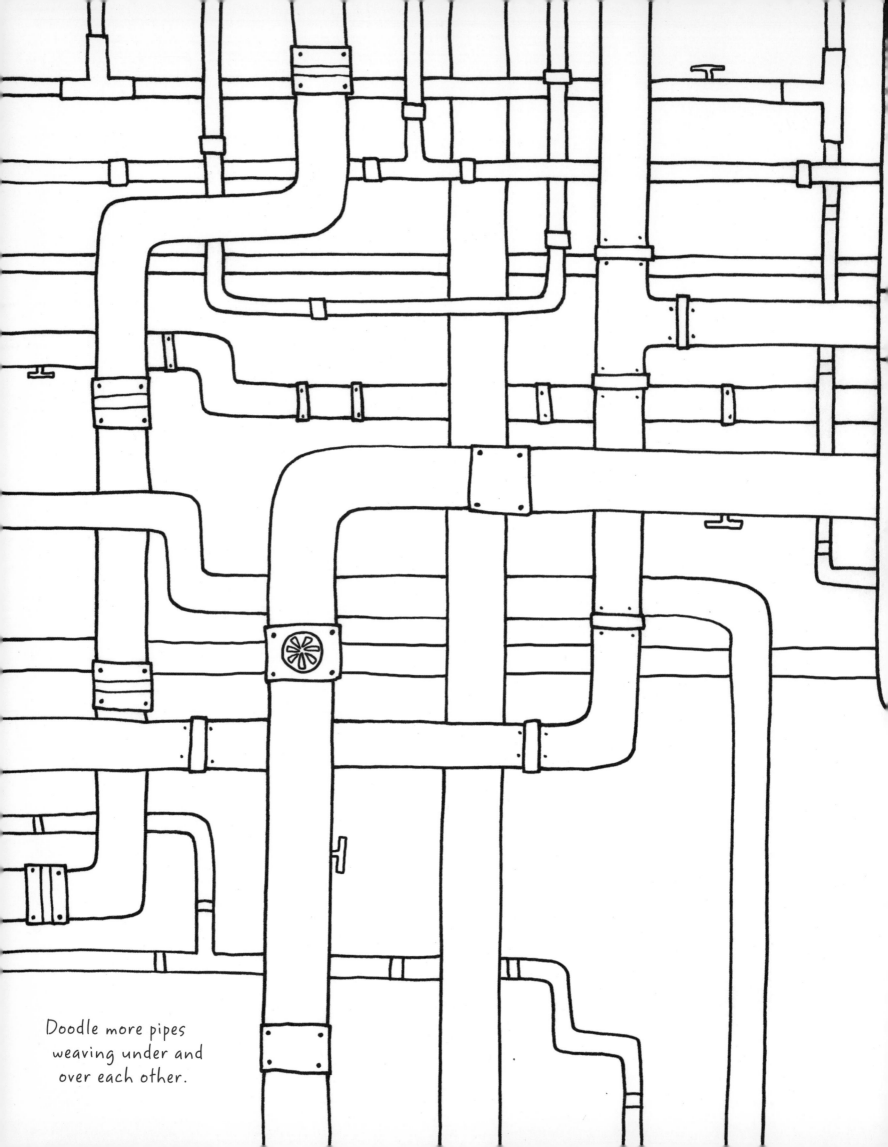

Doodle more pipes
weaving under and
over each other.

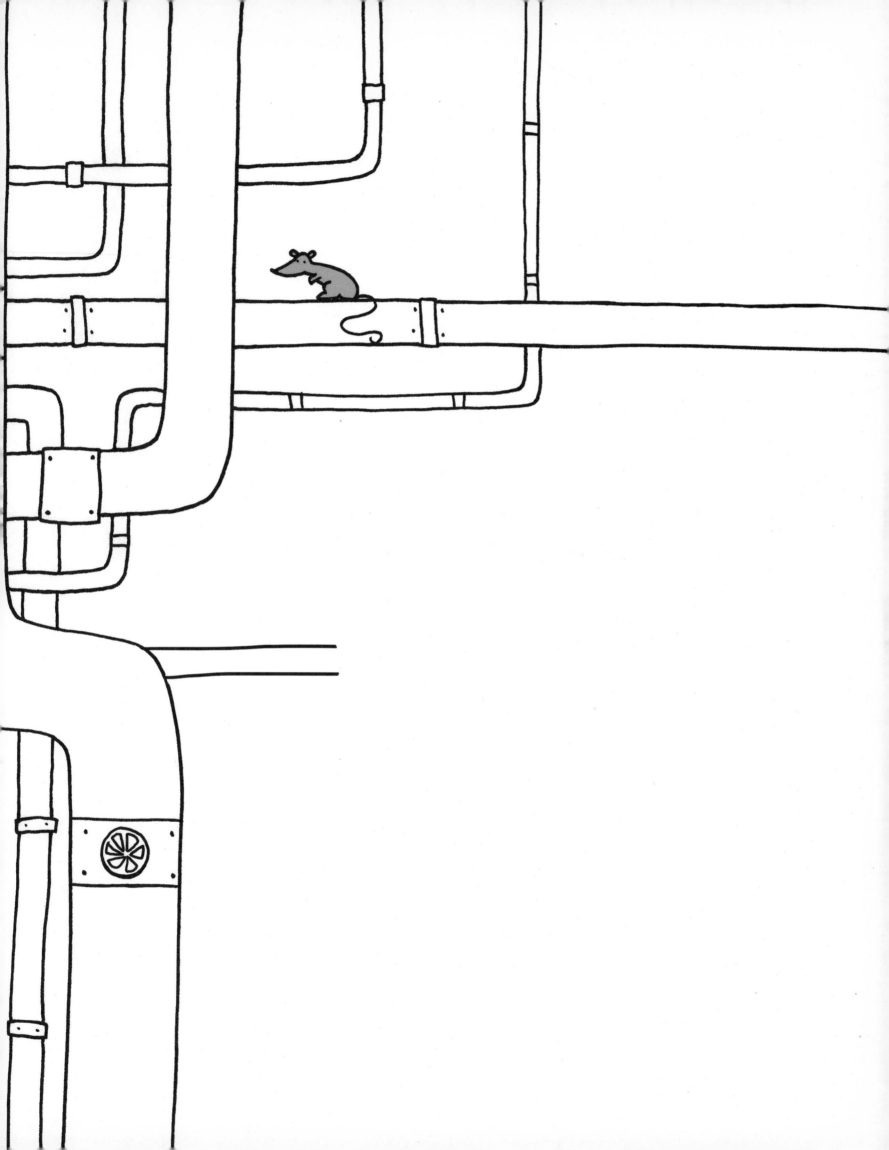

Doodle cats and dogs.

Finish the faces in the crowd.

Fill the pages with bugs, ants and other creepy crawlies.

Fill the trees with doodled leaves.

Draw things in the
windows and washing
on the lines.

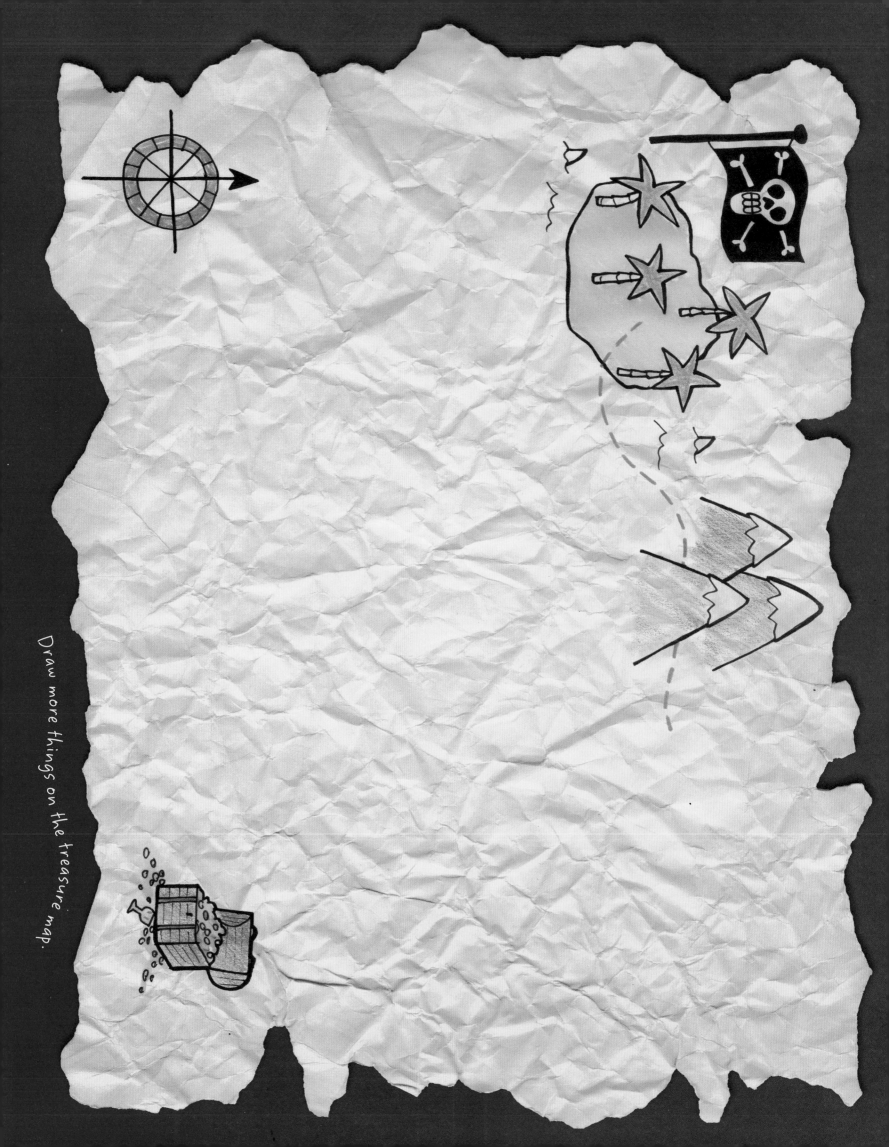

Draw more things on the treasure map.

Draw pointed teeth...

...and add more scales.

Draw more cacti and snakes.

Turn these shapes into monsters.

Draw birds on the branches and leaves on the tree.

Doodle patterns to turn these shapes into snowflakes.

Keep on doodling without taking your pen off the paper.

Add more bats in the trees.

Doodle more swirly patterns.

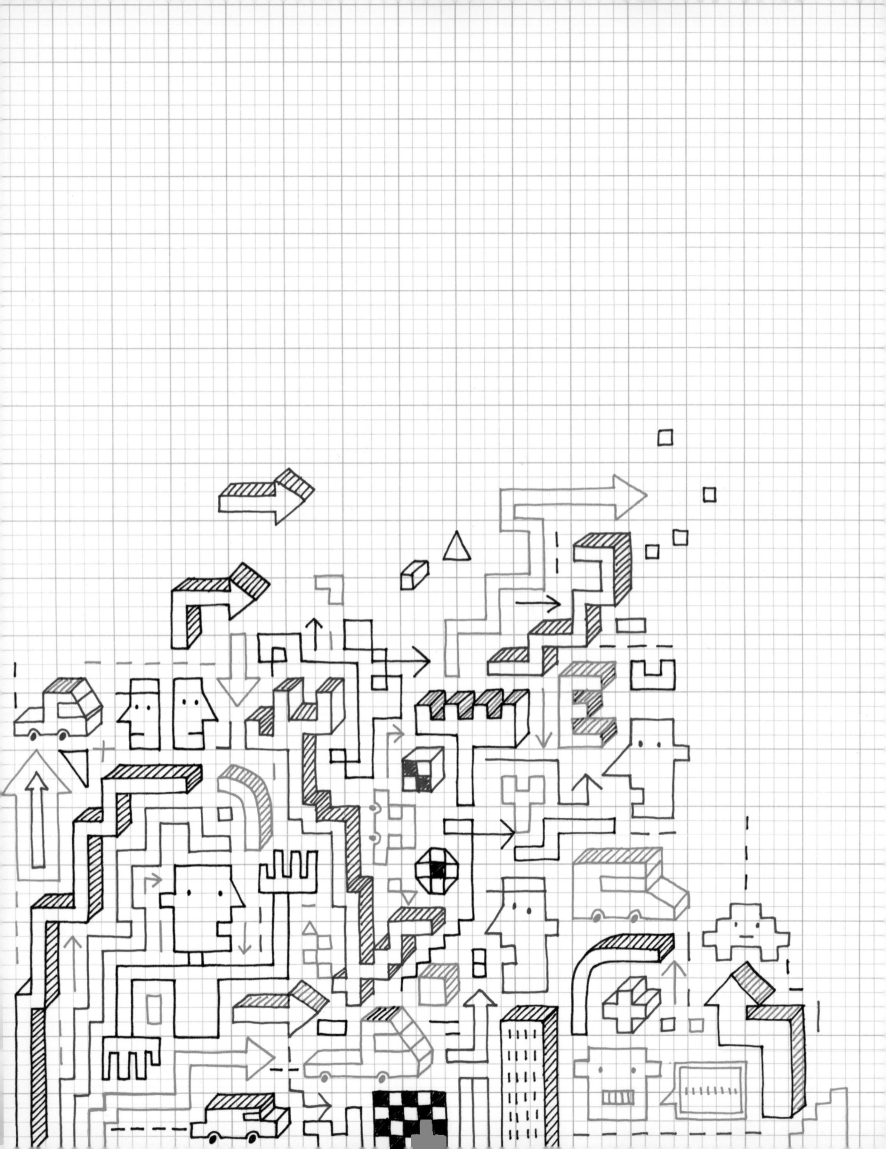

Use the grid lines to draw lots of doodles.

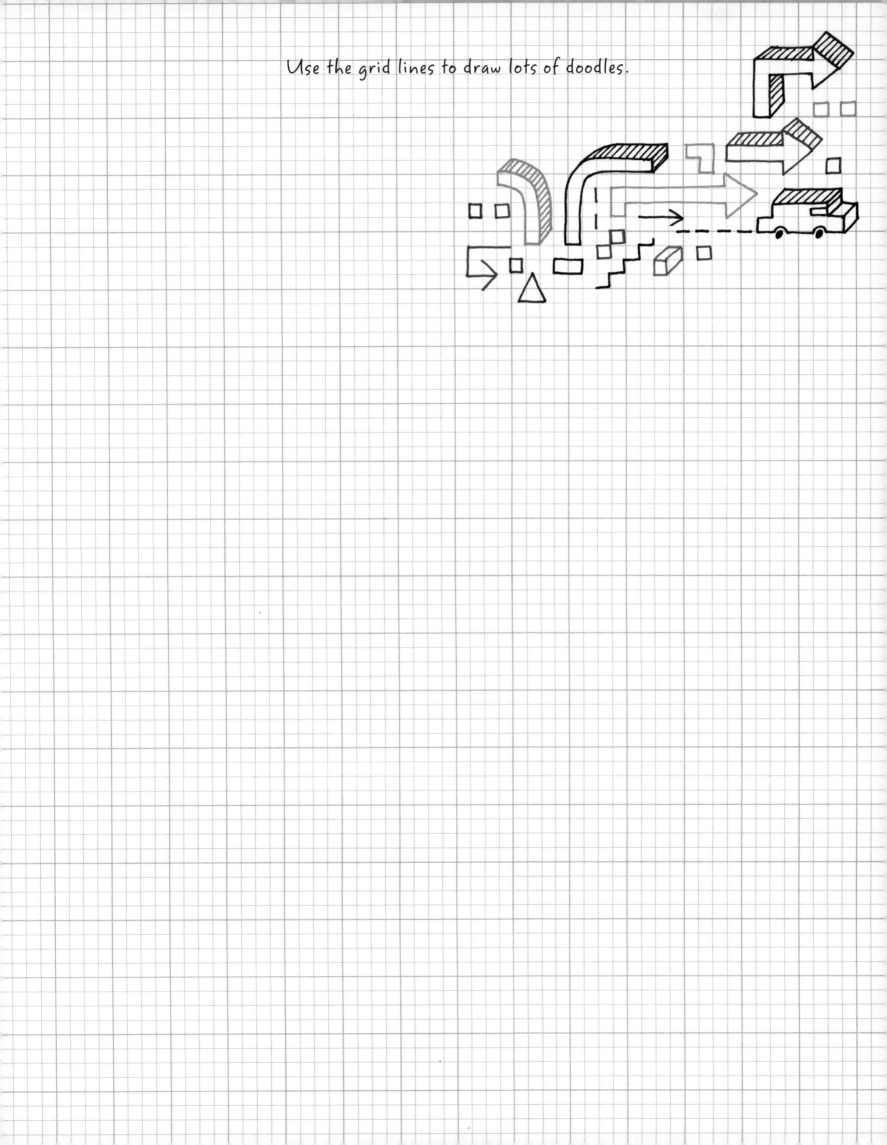

Add patterns on the cars and their wheels.

Doodle more patterns and fill in the shapes.

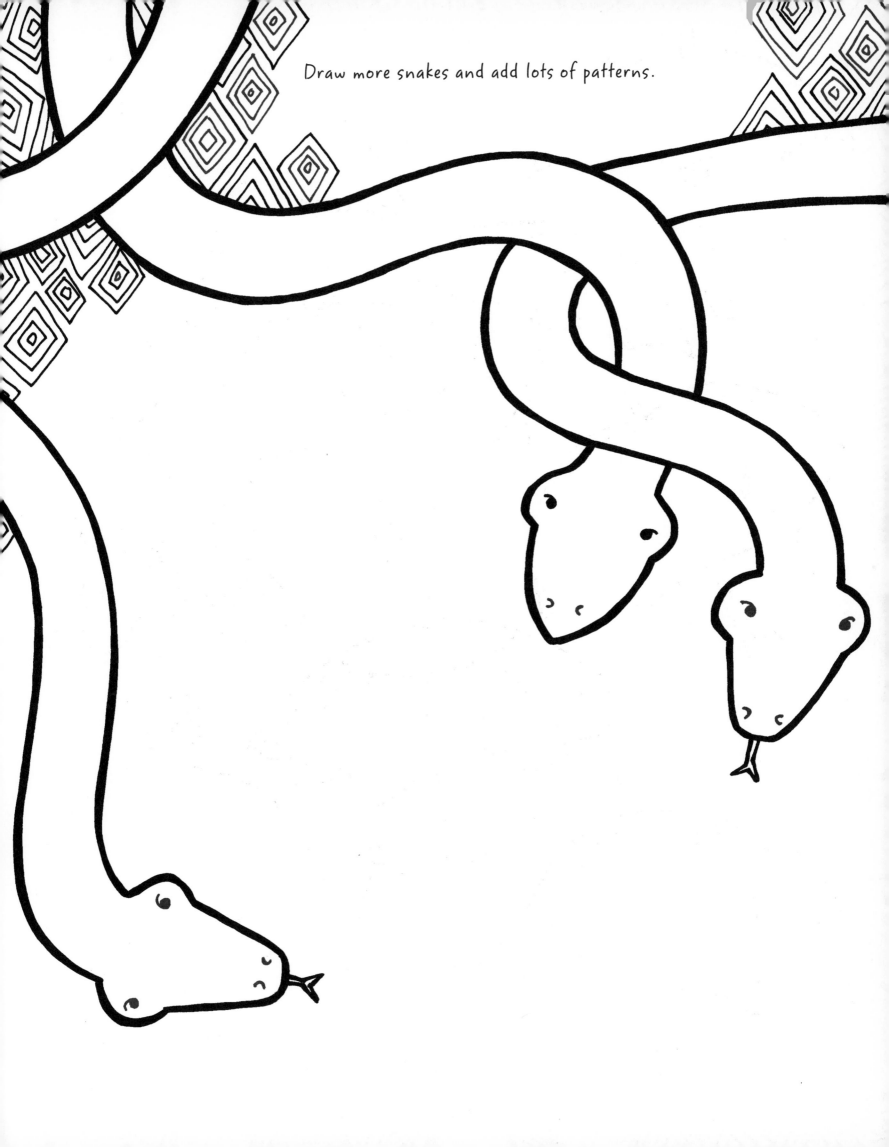

Draw more snakes and add lots of patterns.

Decorate the umbrellas.

Fill the window with cupcakes, pastries and cakes.

OPEN

Shop hours Mon-Sat 9am-6pm

Join the shapes with doodled patterns.

Draw lots more stars and their trails.

Doodle more red and black plants.

Draw towers and turrets on the castle.

Draw more flowers then
add stalks and leaves.

PAR AVION

Madame Belle Dubois
109 rUE DE LA FLEUR
75008 Paris

Doodle on the stamps and envelopes.

Doodle more lanes and vehicles to create a traffic jam.

Scribble lots of fur on the woolly mammoths. Give the figures hair, beards and hairy clothes.

Design some patterns for the beach gear.

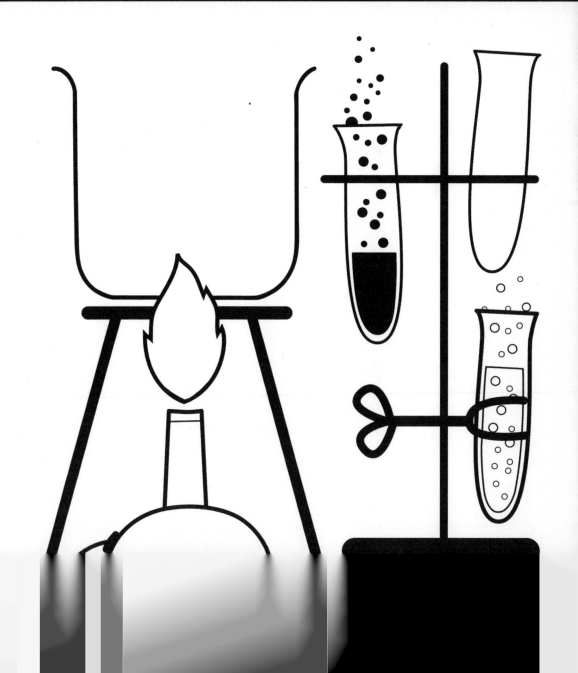

Draw lots more bright tropical fish.

Continue doodling monsters without taking your pen off the paper.

Decorate these cans, jars and boxes, then add some more.

Draw monsters around these eyes.

Draw more monkeys.

Draw the people who are wearing these hats.

Doodle a hat
on each head.

Additional designs by Vicky Arrowsmith.
First published in 2010 by Usborne Publishing Ltd., Usborne House,
83-85 Saffron Hill, London, ECIN 8RT. www.usborne.com © 2010 Usborne
Publishing Ltd. The name Usborne and the devices ♀♥ are Trademarks of
Usborne Publishing Ltd.
 UE First published in America 2010.